From Battlefield to Boardroom

Copyright © 2024 Copyright

All rights reserved.

ISBN:
9798327044968

From Battlefield to Boardroom

DEDICATION

"To all leaders who commit to perpetual growth—this book is dedicated to your endless pursuit of excellence."

From Battlefield to Boardroom

CONTENTS

	Introduction	Pg 6
1	Understanding Situational Leadership and Followership	Pg 9
2	Military Leadership Context	Pg 17
3	Transitioning to Civilian Leadership	Pg 26
4	Applying Situational Leadership in Civilian Settings	Pg 33
5	Tools and Techniques for Situational Leadership	Pg 42
6	Overcoming Challenges and Pitfalls	Pg 50
7	Reflecting on the Journey: Lessons and Insights for Future Leadership	Pg 63
	Conclusion: Beyond the Horizon	Pg 72
	Acknowledgments	Pg 74
	About the Author:	Pg 76

From Battlefield to Boardroom

Introduction:

In the complex landscape of leadership, the transition from military service to civilian leadership roles represents a formidable yet enriching journey. Guided by the wisdom and expertise of Dr. Sigel, President and CEO of Walsh College in Troy, MI, and the steadfast support of his wife, Kyra, Jordan Staub leads the transformative exploration into military situational leadership and how it can be applied to civilian management in "From Battlefield to Boardroom: Applying Situational Leadership Principles from the Military to Civilian Leadership." With over 14 years of military experience spanning two branches—the Air Force and Army—Jordan brings a wealth of firsthand knowledge and strategic insight to the forefront of this narrative.

In the introductory chapters, Jordan extends a warm invitation to readers, offering a reflective overview of the parallels between military and civilian leadership. Rooted in Jordan's leadership journey from the battlefield to the boardroom, the book introduces the foundational principles of situational leadership, acknowledging the seminal contributions of Hersey and Blanchard. Their collaborative effort seamlessly weaves together theoretical frameworks with practical wisdom, setting the stage for a comprehensive exploration of leadership dynamics.

Subsequent chapters delve into the intricacies of military leadership structures, drawing upon Jordan's experiences and insights as a seasoned veteran. From navigating hierarchical command structures to grappling with the unique challenges of military leadership, the narrative unfolds with depth and clarity. Jordan's firsthand accounts of leadership in combat scenarios and training exercises offer readers a vivid glimpse into the complexities of situational leadership within military contexts.

As the narrative transitions to civilian leadership, Jordan navigate the challenges and opportunities inherent in this pivotal transition. Drawing upon his experience as a Senior Technical Writer for the federal government and leading large-scale projects, the book illuminates the nuances of adapting military leadership experiences to fit civilian environments. Through candid reflections and practical guidance, readers gain invaluable insights into the key differences between military and civilian leadership contexts, paving the way for a seamless transition.

Moreover, "From Battlefield to Boardroom" transcends theoretical discourse to offer actionable strategies for implementing situational leadership in civilian settings. With a focus on practical tools, role-playing exercises, and real-world case studies, Jordan empower readers to navigate the complexities of leadership adaptation with confidence and clarity. Their collective expertise serves as a beacon of guidance, inspiring readers to embrace the transformative potential of situational leadership in their own leadership journeys.

As the narrative unfolds, Jordan weave together a tapestry of case studies and success stories, showcasing the transformative power of situational leadership in diverse organizational contexts. His effort serves as a testament to the enduring legacy of military service and its profound insights for leadership in civilian life. Through his passion for leadership excellence, Jordan extends a warm invitation to readers to embark on a journey of discovery, empowerment, and leadership excellence.

Chapter 1:

Understanding Situational Leadership and Followership

In this foundational chapter, we delve into a comprehensive examination of situational leadership, uncovering its definition, principles, and practical applications. Situational leadership, a dynamic approach to leading, underscores the significance of adapting one's leadership style not only to the demands of the situation and the capabilities of the team but also to the principles of effective followership. At its essence, situational leadership acknowledges that leadership is not a static endeavor but rather a fluid process that requires leaders to fluidly adjust their strategies based on the unique circumstances they face, as well as the readiness and responsiveness of their followers.

Understanding Followership: As a soldier, we are instilled with the fundamental principle that effective leadership is intricately linked with mastering followership. In military training, we learn that to lead effectively, one must first understand and excel in the role of a follower. This concept emphasizes the importance of empathy, communication, and teamwork. By experiencing followership firsthand, leaders gain valuable insights into the needs, perspectives, and challenges faced by those they lead.

For instance, during my time in basic training, I vividly remember how our drill instructors exemplified leadership through their actions. They led by example, guiding us through tactical drills and marching exercises. Through the process of shadowing them, we not only absorbed their techniques but also gradually shed any ineffective habits while imbibing healthier ones.

While the intensity of being "smoked" or rigorously disciplined for errors initially seemed harsh, it served a crucial purpose. It simulated the pressure and chaos of real-world scenarios, pushing us to swiftly and accurately make decisions under stress. In essence, these experiences, though challenging, were pivotal in honing our ability to navigate high-pressure situations effectively.

As we compounded these experiences over time, a culture of followership began to take root. We learned not only to follow orders but also to internalize the ethos of teamwork, discipline, and adaptability. This gradual immersion into the rigors of military training not only shaped us as soldiers but also instilled in us the essential qualities of followership, paving the way for our eventual evolution as capable leaders.

In mastering followership, soldiers learn to follow commands with diligence, adaptability, and integrity. They cultivate the ability to support the mission and the team, even in the face of adversity. By demonstrating commitment, discipline, and loyalty as followers, soldiers not only contribute to the success of their units but also develop essential qualities that form the foundation of effective leadership.

Moreover, mastering followership fosters mutual respect and trust between leaders and their teams. Soldiers who excel in followership inspire confidence in their leadership abilities and earn the respect of their peers and superiors. This trust is essential for cohesive teamwork, mission accomplishment, and unit morale.

In essence, the mastery of followership is not just a precursor to leadership; it is a continuous journey that shapes the character, competence, and credibility of every effective leader in the military and beyond.

Followership and situational leadership share a symbiotic relationship crucial for effective leadership within organizations, including the military. In the realm of situational leadership, leaders must adapt their style to suit the situation and the readiness level of their followers. Conversely, effective followership necessitates individuals to adapt to the leadership style provided by their leaders. This mutual adaptability fosters a harmonious interaction between leaders and followers, enhancing organizational effectiveness. Moreover, effective followership involves understanding and responding to the goals, expectations, and communication styles of leaders, mirroring the emphasis in situational leadership on leaders understanding their followers' needs and abilities. This reciprocal understanding forms the basis for a feedback loop, where followers provide input to leaders about the impact of their leadership style, fostering collaboration and trust. Ultimately, the synergy between followership and situational leadership promotes teamwork, collaboration, and dynamic leadership within organizations, exemplifying their complementary nature in the realm of effective leadership.

Understanding Situational Leadership Model (SLM): The Situational Leadership Model (SLM), developed by Paul Hersey and Ken Blanchard, provides a structured framework for understanding and applying situational leadership principles. At the heart of the SLM are two key dimensions: leadership behavior and follower readiness. Leadership behavior refers to the style of leadership employed by the leader, which can range from directing to delegating. Follower readiness, on the other hand, refers to the ability and willingness of the followers to perform a given task.

According to the SLM, effective leadership involves matching the leadership style to the level of follower readiness. For example, when followers are highly capable and motivated, a delegating style of leadership may be most appropriate, as it empowers followers to take ownership of tasks and make decisions independently. Conversely, when followers are inexperienced or unsure, a directing style of leadership may be necessary to provide clear guidance and support.

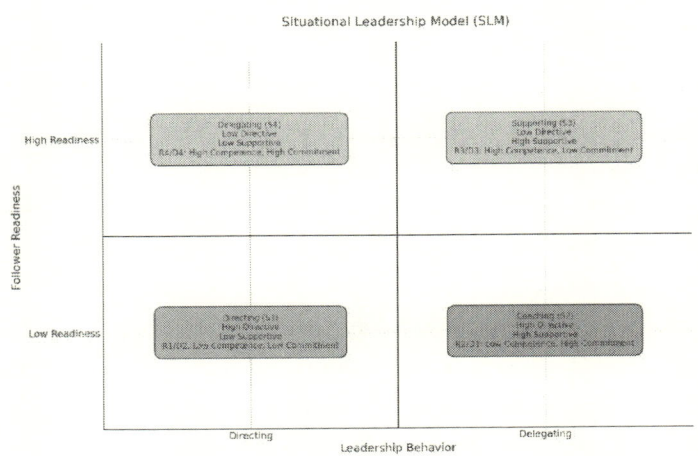

Figure 1.

The SLM framework figure above explores the comprehensive dynamics of situational leadership, incorporating both task readiness and psychological development of followers. Task readiness, rephrased as task development by Blanchard, encompasses the skills, knowledge, and abilities essential for executing assigned tasks, emphasizing continual growth in followers' capabilities over time. Psychological readiness, renamed psychological development, pertains to followers' willingness to assume responsibility for their actions, reflecting their motivation, drive, and confidence. Blanchard substitutes competence for ability and commitment for willingness in his terminology.

Blanchard's model delineates four follower styles, each denoted by a combination of task and psychological readiness levels. R1 (D2) followers lack both competence and commitment, while R2 (D1) followers exhibit willingness despite lacking competence, often observed in new employees eager to impress. R3 (D3) followers possess competence but lack commitment, potentially due to motivational issues or apprehension about performing tasks independently. R4 (D4) followers demonstrate both high competence and commitment, representing the pinnacle of readiness.

Blanchard's approach to situational leadership involves adjusting directive and supportive behaviors according to followers' readiness levels. The leader's directive behavior, emphasizing task accomplishment, should align with followers' developmental stages. Supportive behavior, focusing on fostering relationships, should similarly correspond to followers' readiness levels. Four leadership styles—Telling (S1), Selling (S2), Participating (S3), and Delegating (S4)—vary in their balance of directive and supportive behaviors, tailored to meet followers' evolving needs. Blanchard and Hersey diverge from theories advocating a singular leadership style, advocating instead for adaptive leadership approaches contingent upon situational demands, thereby contributing to the broader discourse on situational and contingency theories of leadership.

Flexibility and adaptability are essential components of situational leadership. Effective leaders must be able to assess the needs of the situation and adjust their leadership approach accordingly. This may require shifting between different leadership styles as the situation evolves or as the needs of the team change over time. By remaining flexible and adaptable, leaders can better meet the needs of their followers and maximize their potential for success.

Closing: As we conclude this chapter, it becomes apparent that the principles of situational leadership extend far beyond theoretical frameworks, finding practical application in diverse real-world scenarios. Thus, it is imperative that we uphold flexibility and adaptability as guiding principles to navigate the dynamic and ever-changing landscape of reality. From military commanders guiding troops into battle to corporate executives steering teams through periods of change, these individuals exemplify the versatility and effectiveness inherent in situational leadership. With a grasp of these fundamental principles, readers stand ready to navigate the intricacies of leadership, propelling success and nurturing advancement within their respective organizations and teams.

Chapter 2:
Military Leadership Context

In the military, the environment operates at a rapid pace, characterized by constant change and sporadic encounters with chaos. Adhering strictly to one leadership style is a treacherous path; instead, it's crucial to remain fluid and adaptable, capable of embracing traits of followership when necessary and selecting the most suitable leadership approach for prevailing conditions. As Bruce Lee famously advised, "Be water, my friend."

In this pivotal chapter, we explore the unique dynamics and challenges of military leadership, drawing upon insights from both personal experiences and scholarly research.

Leveraging both negative and positive experiences as lessons: Throughout my tenure in the military, I've encountered both exemplary and deficient leadership, each leaving a profound impact on my journey toward becoming a better leader. The negative experiences have served as invaluable lessons on what not to do as a leader, reinforcing the importance of empathy and understanding from the follower's perspective. The positive experiences serve as a blueprint for equipping myself with the necessary tools to become an effective leader. By internalizing these lessons, I've enhanced my emotional intelligence, equipping myself with a deeper understanding of effective leadership practices and paving the way for more impactful leadership in the future.

In my time with the Air Force, I encountered a situation that tested the balance between duty and personal emergency. One morning, just before a scheduled drill, a severe storm had knocked down high voltage power lines into my backyard. Concerned for the safety of my wife and children, I promptly contacted my branch chief, a Senior Master Sergeant, to inform him of the emergency and to ensure it was acceptable for me to briefly delay my arrival at the drill to address this hazard. He gave me permission to take the necessary time to secure my family's safety and to contact DTE Energy to handle the fallen lines. Remarkably, I managed to resolve the situation and arrive only 15 minutes late to the drill, a feat I found impressively efficient given the circumstances.

However, despite the prior approval and my quick handling of the situation, the Senior Master Sergeant did not share my perspective. Instead, he issued me a Letter of Counseling (LOC) for my tardiness. He acknowledged that while he had initially permitted the delay, the expectation to prioritize military duties remained paramount, underscoring a strict interpretation of protocol regardless of the circumstances.

The incident with the Senior Master Sergeant, while frustrating, underscored the complexity of leadership in the military and in general. It illuminated the stark differences between administrative adherence and situational leadership. Such experiences, particularly the LOC, have driven home the importance of flexibility and the need to adapt leadership styles to the nuances of each situation. As I reflect on this incident and others like it, we are reminded of the delicate balance leaders must maintain between enforcing standards and responding humanely to unforeseen circumstances.

This balance is critical not only in handling emergencies but also in everyday leadership. True leadership requires a nuanced approach that considers the human element. It involves understanding that behind every decision, there are personal stakes involved. By integrating the lessons learned from both positive and negative leadership examples, we aim to foster an environment that values both discipline and empathy, ensuring that the needs of the mission and the well-being of the personnel are both adequately addressed. This approach not only enhances the effectiveness of the team but also cultivates a culture of respect and understanding, paving the way for a more adaptive and responsive leadership style.

Overview of Military Leadership Structure and Hierarchy: In our exploration of military leadership structures, we delve into the hierarchical command systems that define military organizations. Understanding the chain of command and the distinct roles of noncommissioned officers (NCOs) and commissioned officers is crucial to grasping the structured framework that governs military leadership. Through personal insights from my service in the Air National Guard and Army Reserves, I aim to illuminate the nuances of military rank, authority, and responsibility.

The hierarchical command within the Air National Guard and Army Reserves emphasizes clear lines of authority and accountability, stretching from the highest echelons down to individual soldiers. A key aspect of this structure is the role of NCOs and commissioned officers, each of whom plays a critical part in both operational decisions and the day-to-day management of military personnel.

NCOs, often considered the backbone of the military, are directly responsible for the management of enlisted personnel. They play a pivotal role in bridging the gap between the enlisted ranks and commissioned officers, not just in tactical field operations but also in substantial mentoring responsibilities. Their influence extends into the everyday lives and professional development of the soldiers under their command.

Conversely, commissioned officers, who are granted legal authority by their commission, handle higher-level strategic planning and leadership responsibilities. These officers are tasked with making decisions that significantly impact military strategy and operational effectiveness. Their roles demand a deep understanding of military dynamics and the ability to lead large groups of personnel towards achieving strategic objectives.

By examining both the enlisted and officer ranks, we observe a structured progression that enhances organizational efficiency and discipline. Enlisted ranks, beginning at the entry level and advancing through to senior levels, are primarily focused on operational roles and technical expertise. Officer ranks, starting from junior officers to senior leaders, are increasingly involved with strategic planning and leadership.

This tiered structure of command and the dynamic between the different ranks form the backbone of military efficiency and discipline, ensuring that every member of the military understands their role and the expectations set upon them. It's a system designed to maintain order and facilitate clear communication across all levels, proving essential for successful military operations and leadership development.

Discussion of Unique Challenges: Military leadership presents a distinct set of challenges, ranging from the physical demands of combat to the psychological pressures of decision-making in high-stakes environments. Through firsthand accounts and case studies, we gain a deep appreciation for the complexities of leading troops in dynamic and unpredictable situations. We explore the concept of VUCA (volatility, uncertainty, complexity, and ambiguity) and its implications for military leadership, highlighting the importance of adaptability, resilience, and strategic thinking in overcoming challenges.

The unique challenges faced by military leaders are multifaceted and intense, demanding a high level of adaptability and resilience. The VUCA (volatility, uncertainty, complexity, and ambiguity) environment in which military operations occur requires leaders to continuously adapt their strategies and approaches. This dynamic battlefield scenario not only tests physical endurance but also mental agility in making critical decisions under pressure.

The military not only faces the challenge of operating within chaotic environments but also confronts the complexities of diversity. Serving as a cultural melting pot, the military comprises service members from across the nation and around the globe. This diversity was particularly evident during my deployment in Operation Enduring Freedom, where my unit included individuals from diverse backgrounds ranging from Africa to the southern United States while I brought my own Northern perspective from Michigan. Each member brought unique subcultural influences that shaped their behaviors and perspectives.

Throughout my seven-month deployment in the desert, it became clear that these varied perspectives were not just background noise; they were pivotal to our operational success. By viewing our diversity in culture and thought as an asset, we leveraged our collective insights to approach problems differently than most units might. This ability to integrate diverse viewpoints enabled us to adapt and innovate, turning potential chaos into strategic advantages. In such dynamic and unpredictable settings, the varied backgrounds of our team members enriched our discussions, leading to innovative solutions that might not have emerged in a more homogenous group. This experience underscored that in the military, diversity is not merely about representation—it's a vital component of our strength and adaptability.

This perspective — viewing diversity as a strength and skillfully blending different subcultures — is a cornerstone of effective situational leadership. Recognizing and utilizing the diverse backgrounds and viewpoints of team members not only enhances problem-solving capabilities but also fosters a unified and adaptive team environment. Embracing this approach enables leaders to effectively navigate complex situations by harnessing the collective strength of their team's varied experiences and insights.

As explored through various firsthand accounts and case studies within the military community, these challenges often push leaders to develop innovative solutions and foster a deep-seated resilience among their troops. Effective military leadership, therefore, involves not just commanding respect and obedience but also inspiring confidence and fostering teamwork under the most stressful conditions. Leaders must be adept at navigating both the expected and unexpected, often having to recalibrate plans and strategies swiftly in response to evolving threats and opportunities. This ability to manage and lead effectively amidst VUCA conditions exemplifies the essence of military leadership and underscores the importance of a well-rounded and strategic approach to handling the uncertainties of modern warfare.

Closing: By delving into the intricacies of military leadership, we gain a deeper understanding of the unique demands and responsibilities faced by military leaders. Through real-world examples and personal insights, we illuminate the transformative power of situational leadership in driving mission success and fostering resilience in the face of adversity.

Chapter 3:

Transitioning to Civilian Leadership

In this chapter, we delve deeper into the multifaceted process of transitioning from military to civilian leadership roles, exploring the intricacies and challenges faced by veterans as they navigate this transformative journey.

Challenges Faced by Military Veterans: Transitioning from the structured environment of the military to the dynamic landscape of civilian leadership presents a host of unique challenges for veterans. From adjusting to new organizational cultures and communication norms to grappling with unfamiliar performance expectations, veterans must navigate a complex array of hurdles as they transition to civilian roles. We shed light on the emotional and psychological toll of transition, exploring themes of identity loss, role ambiguity, and cultural assimilation. By highlighting the lived experiences of veterans, we aim to provide a deeper understanding of the challenges inherent in transitioning to civilian leadership roles.

The journey from military to civilian life is marked not only by external challenges but also by internal struggles that can profoundly impact a veteran's transition. The shift from a highly structured military environment to the more fluid dynamics of civilian workplaces can be jarring. Veterans often find themselves having to recalibrate their leadership styles and communication methods to fit into less hierarchical and more collaborative civilian settings. This adaptation process can sometimes lead to feelings of alienation and confusion, as the clear-cut roles and identities they once held in the military become blurred in civilian contexts.

Additionally, the skills and leadership experience veterans acquire in the military—highly valued in that context—may not always be understood or appreciated in the civilian sector, leading to underemployment or misalignment in roles that fail to leverage their robust skill sets. As we delve deeper into these themes through personal stories and broader case studies, it becomes evident that supporting veterans in their transition is not just about providing job opportunities but also about ensuring they have the resources to mentally and emotionally navigate the shift. It is crucial for civilian organizations to foster an inclusive environment that respects and integrates the unique backgrounds and skills of veterans, ultimately enriching the organization's culture and enhancing its leadership diversity.

Key Differences Between Military and Civilian

Leadership: Central to successful transition is a nuanced understanding of the fundamental differences between military and civilian leadership contexts. Through a comparative analysis of organizational structures, decision-making processes, and leadership styles, we illuminate the distinct challenges and opportunities presented by each context. From the hierarchical command structures of the military to the collaborative and decentralized nature of civilian organizations, veterans must adapt their leadership approaches to align with the unique demands of the civilian workplace.

Understanding the key differences between military and civilian leadership is essential for veterans transitioning to civilian roles. Military leadership often operates within a strict hierarchy where orders flow downward and adherence to protocols is paramount. In contrast, civilian leadership tends to value collaboration and often features a decentralized decision-making process, where input from various levels can influence outcomes. This shift can pose a significant challenge for veterans who are accustomed to a more structured command environment.

To successfully adapt, veterans need to recalibrate their leadership styles to be more inclusive and participatory, often embracing a more nuanced approach to authority and influence. Real-world examples highlight veterans who have successfully transitioned by leveraging their disciplined backgrounds while learning new interpersonal dynamics to lead diverse teams effectively in civilian settings. Scholarly research further supports these findings, suggesting that veterans who actively seek to understand and integrate into the civilian leadership culture can not only adapt but thrive, bringing valuable perspectives and experiences that enhance their roles as civilian leaders. By examining these transitions, this analysis provides crucial insights for veterans, helping them navigate the complexities of their new environments and capitalize on the opportunities available in civilian leadership positions.

Importance of Adapting Military Leadership Experience: Despite the challenges, military veterans bring a wealth of valuable leadership experiences to civilian roles. Through reflective exercises, we explore strategies for translating military leadership skills and experiences into civilian contexts. From leveraging skills in strategic planning and crisis management to fostering a culture of discipline and accountability, veterans have the opportunity to make significant contributions to their organizations by adapting and applying their military leadership experiences in new and innovative ways. By providing practical guidance and actionable strategies for leveraging military leadership experiences in civilian roles, we empower veterans to embrace their unique talents and capabilities as they embark on their civilian leadership journey.

The transition from military to civilian leadership offers a unique opportunity for civilian leaders to harness military situational leadership skills. Military veterans possess a profound depth of experience in strategic planning, crisis management, and maintaining discipline—skills that can significantly enhance civilian leadership practices. By incorporating these military-derived strategies, civilian leaders can foster a resilient and adaptable organizational culture, capable of thriving under various pressures.

Civilian organizations stand to benefit greatly from adopting a situational leadership approach that emphasizes adaptability and accountability. For example, the military's methodical approach to crisis management involves clear communication, rapid assessment, and decisive action, all of which are invaluable in corporate settings, especially during times of uncertainty or challenge. Furthermore, the disciplined framework that veterans are accustomed to can help in structuring teams in a way that promotes efficiency and accountability.

In fostering this integration, it is crucial for organizations to create environments where the unique perspectives and skills of veterans are valued and leveraged. By conducting workshops and training sessions that focus on translating these military skills to the civilian context, organizations can enable veterans to smoothly transition their leadership capabilities. This not only aids the veterans in their personal adjustment but also enriches the leadership dynamics within the organization, introducing a level of rigor and precision to decision-making processes that is often honed in military settings.

Ultimately, embracing military leadership styles can guide civilian leaders towards more dynamic and robust leadership models, equipping them to handle complex situations with a strategic and disciplined approach. This melding of military precision with civilian flexibility creates a powerful leadership paradigm that enhances the overall effectiveness and adaptability of organizations.

Closing: In conclusion, the transition from military to civilian leadership is both a challenge and an opportunity. It requires veterans to reimagine their well-honed leadership skills in a new context, often demanding significant adjustments in communication style, decision-making processes, and team dynamics. However, the same qualities that define effective military leaders—discipline, resilience, and strategic thinking—can also make them exceptional leaders in civilian roles. By embracing the complexity of this transition and viewing it as an opportunity for growth, veterans can significantly enhance their leadership effectiveness and make invaluable contributions to their new organizations.

This chapter has highlighted the importance of supporting veterans through this transition, not just in finding suitable roles but in recognizing and integrating their unique skills and experiences. For organizations, the integration of veterans into civilian leadership roles is not just about offering employment; it's about enriching the organization's culture and leveraging diverse perspectives that can lead to greater innovation and adaptability.

As we continue to explore and support these transitions, we will undoubtedly uncover even deeper insights into the synergies between military and civilian leadership styles. The journey is complex, but the rewards—both for the veterans themselves and for the organizations that employ them—are profound and impactful, driving success in an ever-evolving business landscape.

Chapter 4:

Applying Situational Leadership in Civilian Settings

In this chapter, we embark on a profound exploration of the practical application of situational leadership principles in civilian workplaces. Situational leadership, a dynamic and adaptive approach to leadership, holds immense potential for transforming organizational dynamics and driving exceptional results. Through a journey of discovery and enlightenment, we delve into the depths of situational leadership, uncovering its profound implications and unveiling its transformative power in the civilian context.

Unveiling the Versatility of Situational Leadership: At the heart of situational leadership lies its unparalleled versatility and adaptability. Unlike traditional leadership approaches that prescribe rigid frameworks and one-size-fits-all solutions, situational leadership embraces the fluidity and complexity of the modern workplace. By acknowledging the unique needs and capabilities of individuals and teams, situational leadership empowers leaders to tailor their approaches to suit the specific demands of each situation. From nurturing emerging talents to guiding seasoned professionals, situational leadership offers a flexible toolkit for navigating the diverse terrain of the civilian workplace with finesse and agility.

Harnessing the Power of Contextual Intelligence: Central to the effective application of situational leadership is the cultivation of contextual intelligence – the ability to discern and respond to the nuances of each situation. Through a deep dive into the principles of contextual intelligence, we illuminate the intricate interplay of factors that shape organizational dynamics, from industry trends and market forces to internal culture and team dynamics. Armed with a keen understanding of the contextual landscape, leaders can adeptly assess the needs and challenges of their teams, leveraging situational leadership principles to chart a course towards success.

To effectively apply situational leadership, cultivating contextual intelligence is crucial. This involves developing the ability to understand and respond to the specific nuances and dynamics of each situation within an organization. Contextual intelligence allows leaders to navigate complex and changing environments by recognizing and interpreting the external and internal factors that impact organizational performance. These factors include market trends, industry shifts, company culture, and team dynamics, each of which plays a critical role in shaping strategic decisions.

1. *Understanding Market Forces and Industry Trends:* Leaders equipped with contextual intelligence are sensitive to the broader economic and social trends that affect their industry. This includes staying informed about technological advancements, competitive strategies, regulatory changes, and market demands. By understanding these external forces, leaders can better anticipate challenges and opportunities for their organization, allowing for more proactive and strategic decision-making.

2. *Navigating Internal Culture and Team Dynamics:* Beyond external factors, contextual intelligence also involves a deep understanding of the internal workings of the organization. This includes recognizing the unique cultures, values, and behaviors within their teams. Leaders must be adept at sensing the morale, motivations, and concerns of their employees, as these can significantly influence productivity and engagement.

3. *Leveraging Situational Leadership Principles:* With a comprehensive understanding of both external and internal factors, leaders can effectively apply situational leadership principles. This means adapting their leadership style to fit the specific

needs of the team and the situation at hand. For instance, a directive style may be necessary when quick decisions are needed in a crisis, while a more participative approach could be better in situations where team input is crucial for problem-solving.

4. *Charting a Course Towards Success:* By integrating their understanding of contextual dynamics with situational leadership approaches, leaders can craft strategies that are both adaptive and forward-thinking. This capability enables them to guide their teams through challenges efficiently and capitalize on emerging opportunities, ultimately steering the organization toward success.

Incorporating contextual intelligence into leadership practices not only enhances a leader's effectiveness but also empowers the organization to thrive in a complex and ever-changing business environment. This approach fosters a culture of agility, where leaders and teams can dynamically adjust to meet the evolving demands of the market and internal landscapes.

Crafting Compelling Case Studies: To bring the concepts of situational leadership to life, we embark on a journey through compelling case studies that showcase its practical application in various industries and organizational settings. From the fast-paced world of technology startups to the complex realm of healthcare management, we explore real-world examples of leaders who have successfully implemented situational leadership principles to drive organizational excellence. Through rich narratives and insightful analysis, readers gain a deeper appreciation for the transformative impact of situational leadership in driving innovation, fostering collaboration, and achieving sustainable growth.

The case of Filentia, a startup focused on providing student finance, showcases the practical application of situational leadership in a technology startup environment. The founders, Tom and Sven, exemplify how diverse backgrounds and skills can effectively complement each other to enhance a company's success. Tom, with his experience in banking and fintech, and Sven, with his background in medicine and startup ventures, combined their distinct skill sets to address complex challenges in the education finance sector.

This case study illustrates the importance of leveraging both hard skills (like industry knowledge and technical expertise) and soft skills (such as adaptability and effective communication) within a startup team. By acknowledging the value of shared leadership rather than a hierarchical model, Filentia's founders were able to foster a collaborative environment that was responsive to the dynamic needs of their business and market.

The success of Filentia underlines a key lesson for applying situational leadership in civilian settings: the integration of diverse skills and perspectives, coupled with a flexible leadership approach, can significantly boost innovation and adaptability in rapidly evolving industries. This aligns with the broader themes of utilizing military situational leadership skills in civilian roles, where the focus is on adapting leadership styles to meet the varied and changing needs of the team and objectives.

You can view the detailed case study of Filentia and its approach to shared leadership within a startup team on the Mastering Entrepreneurship blog by Cambridge Judge Business School.

Citation: Mastering Entrepreneurship at Cambridge Judge. (2019, June 12). Case Study: Filentia – Shared leadership in a startup team. Retrieved from Mastering Entrepreneurship Blog.

Strategies for Success: Armed with a wealth of insights and inspiration, we equip leaders with a comprehensive toolkit of strategies for effectively applying situational leadership in their own workplaces. From fostering a culture of empowerment and accountability to cultivating open channels of communication and feedback, we explore practical strategies for creating an environment where situational leadership can thrive. Through actionable recommendations and thought-provoking exercises, leaders are empowered to harness the full potential of situational leadership to navigate the complexities of the civilian workplace and drive exceptional results.

To effectively implement situational leadership in the workplace and achieve remarkable results, leaders can adopt several strategic approaches. Here are some practical strategies to foster an environment where situational leadership can flourish:

1. *Tailor Leadership to Individual Needs:* Recognize the unique developmental stage of each team member. Adjust your leadership style to match their competence and motivation level. This may range from more directive approaches for less experienced team members to more delegative styles for those who are more skilled and self-reliant.

2. *Empower and Delegate*: Encourage autonomy by delegating tasks that fit team members' skill levels and career aspirations. This not only empowers them but also builds trust and enhances their confidence in handling responsibilities.

3. *Foster a Culture of Accountability:* Establish clear expectations and hold team members accountable for their contributions. Accountability frameworks should be transparent and consistently applied, ensuring all team members understand their roles and the standards to which they are held.

By integrating these strategies into their leadership approach, leaders can effectively utilize situational leadership principles to navigate complex workplace dynamics and lead their teams to success. These strategies help build a robust framework within which teams can operate efficiently while also adapting to the evolving business landscape.

Closing: As we conclude our exploration of situational leadership in civilian settings, we cast our gaze towards the future, envisioning a world where adaptive leadership approaches are the cornerstone of organizational success. By embracing the principles of situational leadership and cultivating a culture of adaptability and innovation, leaders can navigate the ever-evolving landscape of the modern workplace with confidence and resilience. As we embark on this transformative journey together, let us seize the opportunity to redefine the future of leadership and unlock the boundless potential that lies within each of us.

Chapter 5:

Tools and Techniques for Situational Leadership

In this chapter, we embark on an immersive exploration of the practical tools and techniques that underpin the successful implementation of situational leadership in the civilian workplace. Situational leadership, renowned for its adaptability and versatility, requires a robust toolkit of resources and strategies to effectively navigate the dynamic challenges of the modern organizational landscape. Through a comprehensive examination of proven methodologies and innovative approaches, we equip leaders with the skills and insights needed to master the art of situational leadership and drive exceptional results.

Harnessing Practical Tools for Leadership Success: At the core of effective situational leadership lies a suite of practical tools and methodologies designed to empower leaders to adapt their approaches to suit the needs of each situation. From leadership style assessments to situational analysis frameworks, we unveil a diverse array of tools that enable leaders to diagnose, evaluate, and respond to the unique challenges and opportunities presented by the civilian workplace. By leveraging these tools, leaders can gain invaluable insights into the dynamics of their teams and organizations, guiding their decision-making and fostering a culture of continuous improvement and innovation.

To effectively harness practical tools for leadership success in the realm of situational leadership, this section introduces a variety of tools and methodologies that help leaders adapt their strategies to meet the specific needs of each scenario. These tools are essential for diagnosing, evaluating, and responding to the unique challenges and opportunities within the civilian workplace.

1. *Leadership Style Assessments:* Tools such as the Hersey-Blanchard Situational Leadership Model provide assessments that help leaders identify their default leadership styles. These assessments guide leaders in understanding how their natural tendencies align with the needs of different team dynamics and situations. By recognizing their own leadership styles, leaders can more effectively adjust their approaches to better suit their team's needs.

2. *Situational Analysis Frameworks:* Frameworks like SWOT (Strengths, Weaknesses, Opportunities, Threats) analysis or PESTLE (Political, Economic, Social, Technological, Legal, Environmental) analysis enable leaders to assess

external and internal factors impacting their organizations. These tools help leaders visualize the broader context of their operational environment, making it easier to tailor their strategies to current realities.

3. *Adaptive Leadership Tools:* Tools such as adaptive cycle models, which consist of observing, interpreting, designing, and acting, encourage leaders to remain flexible and responsive. These cycles promote a continuous loop of feedback and adaptation, which is crucial for situational leadership.

4. *Emotional Intelligence (EI) Metrics:* Since situational leadership heavily relies on interpersonal relations, tools that measure and enhance emotional intelligence can be highly beneficial. EI metrics help leaders understand and manage their own emotions and those of their team members, which is vital for effective leadership in varied situations.

5. *Real-Time Feedback Mechanisms:* Implementing technologies that allow for real-time feedback, such as mobile apps or online platforms, can dramatically enhance the immediacy and

relevance of feedback, allowing leaders to quickly adjust their methods in response to team input.

6. *Scenario Planning Tools:* These tools enable leaders to simulate different leadership challenges and outcomes based on varying conditions. By engaging with scenario planning, leaders can develop a range of responses to potential future situations, which is a key component of effective situational leadership.

By integrating these tools into their leadership practices, leaders are not only equipped to handle the complexities of their roles more effectively but are also positioned to drive continual improvement and innovation within their teams. The use of these diverse tools enables leaders to develop a nuanced understanding of their organizational dynamics and craft approaches that are precisely aligned with their teams' needs and the strategic objectives of their organizations. This proactive and thoughtful application of situational leadership tools ensures that leaders can navigate the complexities of the modern workplace with confidence and insight.

Empowering Ongoing Self-Assessment and Improvement: Continuous self-assessment is the cornerstone of leadership growth and development. In this section, we explore practical strategies for ongoing self-assessment and improvement as a situational leader. From soliciting feedback from peers and subordinates to engaging in reflective practices and seeking out professional development opportunities, leaders can cultivate a mindset of continuous learning and growth. By embracing a culture of self-awareness and self-improvement, leaders can enhance their effectiveness and drive organizational success with confidence and resilience.

Empowering ongoing self-assessment and improvement is vital for situational leaders who wish to excel in their roles and foster a culture of excellence within their organizations. This section provides a series of practical strategies designed to help leaders continuously refine their skills and adapt to evolving leadership demands.

1. *Establishing Regular Feedback Mechanisms:* Leaders should establish structured processes for receiving regular feedback from peers, subordinates, and supervisors. This could involve 360-degree feedback systems that offer comprehensive insights into how a leader's style is perceived across different levels of the organization. Regular performance reviews and real-time feedback using digital tools can also provide continuous insights and opportunities for growth.

2. *Reflective Practice:* Encouraging leaders to engage in reflective practices is crucial. This might involve maintaining a leadership journal, where leaders can reflect on their daily experiences, challenges faced, and lessons learned. Reflective practice helps leaders make sense of complex situations and enhances their decision-making skills.

3. *Professional Development Plans:* Leaders should develop and regularly update their professional development plans. These plans should be aligned with their career goals and the strategic objectives of the organization. Including specific milestones and timelines, these plans can guide leaders in pursuing relevant courses, workshops, and seminars that enhance their leadership capabilities.

4. *Utilizing Technology for Self-Assessment:* Leaders can leverage technology to enhance their self-assessment practices. Apps and online platforms offer various resources, including personality tests, leadership style assessments, and skill-tracking tools, which can provide leaders with ongoing insights into their professional growth and areas needing improvement.

5. *Mentorship and Coaching:* Participating in mentorship programs, either as mentors or mentees, can be highly beneficial. Leaders can also seek out coaching from experienced professionals who can provide guidance, challenge their thinking, and support their development. This relationship provides a safe space for leaders to explore their strengths and weaknesses and receive tailored advice on leadership challenges.

6. *Peer Learning Groups:* Creating or joining peer learning groups can facilitate shared learning experiences. These groups provide a platform for leaders to exchange ideas, discuss common challenges, and support each other's growth through collaborative learning and mutual accountability.

7. *Committing to Lifelong Learning:* A commitment to lifelong learning should be at the heart of every leader's development strategy. This involves staying updated with the latest leadership theories and practices, participating in industry conferences, and continuously seeking

knowledge that can enhance one's leadership approach.

By integrating these strategies into their routine, leaders not only foster their own growth but also set a powerful example for others in the organization. Cultivating a mindset of continuous learning and self-improvement ensures that leaders are well-equipped to adapt their leadership styles to meet the needs of their teams and drive organizational success effectively.

Closing: As we conclude our exploration of tools and techniques for situational leadership, we cast our gaze towards the future, envisioning a world where leadership excellence is the hallmark of organizational success. By equipping leaders with the practical tools and strategies needed to excel in their roles, we empower them to cultivate a culture of leadership excellence within their teams and organizations. Through a commitment to continuous learning and improvement, leaders can unleash the full potential of their teams, driving innovation, collaboration, and performance to new heights. As we embark on this transformative journey together, let us embrace the power of situational leadership to shape a brighter future for ourselves and those we lead.

Chapter 6:

Overcoming Challenges and Pitfalls

In this chapter, we confront the common challenges and pitfalls encountered when applying situational leadership principles in the civilian workplace. While situational leadership offers a versatile framework for navigating the complexities of organizational dynamics, it is not without its obstacles. Through a candid exploration of the barriers and stumbling blocks that leaders may encounter, we arm readers with strategies for overcoming resistance to change and implementing new leadership approaches with confidence and resilience.

Identifying Common Challenges: Situational leadership requires leaders to navigate a myriad of challenges, from resistance to change to communication breakdowns and power struggles. In this section, we shine a spotlight on the common pitfalls that leaders may encounter on their journey towards mastering situational leadership. By acknowledging and understanding these challenges, leaders can proactively anticipate and address them, mitigating their impact on organizational effectiveness and success.

To effectively address the challenges of

situational leadership in the civilian workplace, it is crucial to understand and navigate the specific hurdles that may arise. This involves a deeper analysis of the common obstacles and developing strategies to overcome them.

Common Challenges of Situational Leadership:

1. *Resistance to Change:* One of the most significant challenges in implementing situational leadership is the inherent resistance to change found in many organizations. Employees may be comfortable with the status quo and wary of new leadership styles or changes in management practices. Leaders need to be adept at managing change, ensuring that they communicate the benefits clearly and engage their teams throughout the process.

2. *Communication Breakdowns:* Effective communication is the cornerstone of situational leadership, as it involves adjusting leadership styles based on the context and needs of the team members. Breakdowns in communication can lead to misunderstandings and a lack of clarity about roles and expectations, which can impede the effectiveness of leadership efforts.

3. *Power Struggles:* As leaders adapt their styles to different situations, they may face power struggles either from within the team or with other leaders who have different views on handling situations. These struggles can undermine leadership efforts and create a toxic work environment if not managed carefully.

Strategies for Overcoming Challenges:

To overcome these challenges, leaders can adopt several strategic approaches:

1. *Building a Change-Ready Culture:* Cultivate an organizational culture that values flexibility and continuous improvement. This can be achieved by regularly discussing the benefits of change and demonstrating how new approaches can lead to better outcomes. Celebrating small wins from changes can also help in building momentum.

2. *Enhancing Communication Skills:* Leaders should focus on enhancing their communication skills to ensure that messages are clear and tailored to the audience. This might include training on active listening, non-verbal communication, and

emotional intelligence to better understand and respond to team members' cues.

3. *Managing Conflict Effectively:* Develop conflict resolution skills to manage power struggles constructively. This includes understanding different conflict styles, fostering an environment where diverse opinions are valued, and using mediation techniques to handle disputes.

4. *Engaging and Empowering Team Members:* Actively engage team members in decision-making processes, especially during transitions. Empower them by delegating authority and encouraging autonomy, which can help in reducing resistance to leadership changes.

5. *Continuous Learning and Adaptation:* Encourage a mindset of continuous learning and adaptation, both at the individual and organizational levels. Leaders should be open to feedback and willing to adjust their approaches based on what works best in different situations.

By addressing these challenges head-on with well-thought-out strategies, leaders can enhance their ability to apply situational leadership principles effectively, leading to improved team performance and organizational success. This approach not only helps in navigating the complexities of modern organizational dynamics but also ensures that leadership practices are responsive and adaptive to the needs of the team and the broader organizational goals.

Strategies for Overcoming Resistance to Change: Effective leadership involves navigating change and overcoming resistance. Drawing upon insights from change management literature and organizational psychology, we offer practical strategies for overcoming resistance to change and implementing new leadership approaches. From fostering a culture of openness and transparency to involving stakeholders in the decision-making process, leaders can proactively address resistance and build buy-in for new initiatives, driving successful organizational change.

To effectively overcome resistance to change and successfully implement new leadership approaches, drawing upon established principles from change management literature and organizational psychology is essential. Here are some practical strategies to help leaders navigate these challenges:

1. *Communication and Transparency:* Open and honest communication is crucial for managing resistance to change. Leaders should strive to communicate the reasons behind changes, the expected benefits, and any potential impacts on the team. Transparency not only builds trust but also reduces uncertainties that can fuel resistance.

2. *Involving Stakeholders:* Engaging key stakeholders in the planning and decision-making processes can significantly reduce resistance. When team members feel they have a voice in the process and that their input is valued, they are more likely to support and commit to the change. This can be facilitated through workshops, meetings, and regular updates that keep stakeholders informed and involved.

3. *Highlighting Early Wins:* Demonstrating the benefits of change early in the process can help to build momentum and convince skeptics. Highlighting early successes reassures the team that the change is beneficial and encourages continued support moving forward.

4. *Creating a Culture of Flexibility and Learning:* Cultivating an organizational culture that values

flexibility and continuous learning can make adapting to change a more natural process. Encouraging innovation and experimentation can help to foster an environment where change is not only accepted but embraced.

5. *Using Change Agents:* Identifying and empowering change agents within the organization can be a powerful strategy. These are individuals who have influence within the team and are enthusiastic about the change. They can act as champions, helping to spread positive messages and influence their peers.

By employing these strategies, leaders can effectively manage resistance to change and ensure the successful implementation of new initiatives. Each strategy helps to create an environment where change is viewed as an opportunity for growth and improvement rather than a threat to stability and comfort.

Embracing the Power of Communication and Transparency: Effective communication is the lifeblood of organizational success. In this section, we explore the transformative power of communication and transparency in overcoming leadership challenges. By fostering open and honest communication channels, leaders can build trust, foster collaboration, and align organizational efforts towards common goals. we highlight the critical role that communication plays in navigating leadership transitions and overcoming resistance to change.

To effectively harness the power of communication and transparency, leaders must prioritize consistent and open dialogue. This section provides actionable strategies to enhance communication within organizations, emphasizing the importance of transparency as a cornerstone of leadership:

1. *Implement Regular Updates:* Establish routine communication practices such as regular meetings, updates, and newsletters to keep all team members informed about organizational developments and changes. This regularity not only keeps everyone aligned but also prevents the spread of misinformation and reduces uncertainty.

2. *Encourage Two-Way Communication:* Foster an environment where feedback is sought and valued from all levels of the organization. Encouraging employees to voice their concerns and suggestions can lead to valuable insights and foster a sense of ownership and engagement.

3. *Leverage Technology:* Utilize technology to enhance communication across the organization. Tools such as intranets, team collaboration software, and project management tools can help ensure that communication is seamless and accessible to everyone, regardless of location.

4. *Promote Transparency in Decision-Making:* Be open about how decisions are made within the organization. This involves explaining the reasons behind decisions, the factors considered, and how they align with the organization's goals. Transparency in decision-making processes can significantly boost trust and reduce resistance to change.

5. *Handle Sensitive Information with Care:* While promoting openness, it's crucial to balance transparency with discretion, especially when handling sensitive information. Leaders should communicate clearly what can be shared and what must remain confidential, ensuring that this practice is consistent and justified.

By embedding these communication strategies into their leadership approach, leaders can build a robust foundation for overcoming challenges and driving organizational success. Effective communication fosters a culture of openness, facilitates smoother transitions, and enables organizations to adapt more quickly to new challenges and opportunities.

Navigating Leadership Transitions with Confidence: As organizations evolve and grow, leadership transitions are inevitable. we offer guidance on navigating leadership transitions with confidence and grace. From succession planning to onboarding new leaders, we explore practical strategies for ensuring continuity and stability during times of change. By embracing a mindset of adaptability and resilience, leaders can navigate leadership transitions with confidence, empowering their teams to thrive amidst uncertainty and change.

Navigating leadership transitions effectively is crucial for maintaining organizational continuity and stability. Here are some practical strategies and guidance to help leaders manage these transitions with confidence and grace:

1. *Succession Planning:* Develop a robust succession plan that identifies potential future leaders within the organization. This plan should include a clear process for identifying and developing talent

through training programs, mentorship, and rotational assignments across different areas of the organization. The goal is to prepare individuals to step into leadership roles seamlessly when the time comes.

2. *Onboarding New Leaders:* Implement a comprehensive onboarding program for new leaders. This should involve not just an introduction to the operational aspects of the organization but also a deep dive into its culture, values, and strategic goals. Pairing new leaders with mentors can facilitate smoother transitions and quicker integration into the team.

3. *Communication Strategy:* Maintain open lines of communication during the transition period. Regular updates about the transition process can help alleviate uncertainties and foster an environment of trust and openness. Engage all stakeholders in discussions about the changes to reassure them of the future direction and how the transition will benefit the organization.

4. *Cultural Integration:* New leaders often bring their own styles and perspectives. It is important to balance these new approaches with the existing

organizational culture. Encourage new leaders to spend time understanding the existing culture and to gradually introduce changes that align with organizational values and goals.

5. *Adaptability and Resilience Training:* Provide training in adaptability and resilience to all leaders within the organization. Change can be challenging, and training leaders to manage their responses to change effectively can help them lead their teams through transitions more successfully.

6. *Support Systems:* Establish support systems for leaders undergoing transitions. This can include access to external coaches, peer support groups, and regular check-ins with higher management to discuss challenges and gather feedback.

7. *Evaluating Impact:* Regularly evaluate the impact of leadership transitions on the organization. This includes assessing staff morale, productivity levels, and overall business performance. Feedback from these evaluations can guide further improvement in the transition process.

By adopting these strategies, organizations can

ensure that leadership transitions are managed effectively, thereby minimizing disruption and positioning new leaders to successfully drive the organization forward in its growth trajectory. These practices not only help in smoothing the transition but also empower the entire team to thrive amidst changes, fostering a resilient organizational culture.

Closing: As we conclude our exploration of overcoming challenges and pitfalls in situational leadership, we underscore the importance of fostering a culture of continuous improvement. By embracing a growth mindset and a commitment to learning and development, leaders can overcome obstacles, drive innovation, and achieve lasting success. As we embark on this transformative journey together, let us embrace the challenges that lie ahead with courage and determination, confident in our ability to overcome adversity and emerge stronger than ever before.

Chapter 7:

Reflecting on the Journey: Lessons and Insights for Future Leadership

As we bring this exploration of situational leadership to a close with our final chapter, "Reflecting on the Journey: Lessons and Insights for Future Leadership," we transition from overcoming challenges to a period of reflection and forward-thinking. This chapter distills the essential lessons drawn from across various organizational contexts and outlines how these insights can be strategically applied to meet future leadership challenges and opportunities. Here, we encapsulate the core principles we've uncovered and propose ways these principles can empower leaders to navigate the evolving landscapes of their respective fields.

Consolidating Learned Wisdom: Consolidating the wisdom gleaned from our exploration of situational leadership across various sectors, we find that its flexibility and adaptability stand out as key factors contributing to leadership effectiveness. This section distills the core insights from the case studies and success stories that have been highlighted throughout the book, providing a cohesive understanding of how situational leadership can be effectively applied in different contexts.

1. *Adaptability to Context:* One of the principal lessons learned is the importance of adapting leadership styles to fit the specific needs and maturity levels of team members. This adaptability helps in addressing the unique challenges and opportunities within corporate enterprises, startups, and non-profit organizations alike.

2. *Communication as a Cornerstone:* Effective communication has repeatedly emerged as a critical tool for successful situational leadership. Leaders who excel in adjusting their communication styles to meet the needs of their team members foster a more inclusive and supportive environment, which is essential for navigating complex organizational dynamics.

3. *Empowerment and Engagement:* Another significant insight is the role of empowerment in driving team performance. Leaders who delegate effectively and encourage autonomy not only boost morale but also enhance productivity by making team members feel valued and trusted.

4. *Learning and Development:* Across various sectors, continuous learning and development emerged as a cornerstone for successful leadership transitions and adaptation. Leaders who prioritize their own and their team's development are better equipped to handle changes and drive innovation within their organizations.

5. *Cultural Sensitivity:* Especially in diverse settings, understanding and integrating into the cultural dynamics of an organization can significantly impact leadership effectiveness. Leaders who are culturally sensitive are more successful in aligning organizational goals with the values and behaviors of their teams.

These consolidated insights underscore the transformative potential of situational leadership when it is applied thoughtfully and strategically. By embracing these principles, leaders can enhance their influence and effectiveness, fostering environments that are not only productive but also adaptive to the changing needs of their organizations. Through these lessons, this section aims to equip readers with a robust framework for applying situational leadership concepts to their own practices, thereby enhancing their ability to lead successfully in an array of settings.

Adapting Leadership for the Future: As we continue to navigate through a landscape marked by rapid technological advancements and shifts in workforce dynamics, the adaptability of leadership remains more crucial than ever. In this section, we focus on the dynamic application of situational leadership principles to meet the challenges that lie ahead. Emphasizing the need for leaders to stay agile, we explore strategies that facilitate adaptability and proactive learning, underscoring the importance of continuous personal and professional development.

1. *Embracing Technological Change:* Leaders must not only keep abreast of technological trends but also be proficient in integrating new tools and technologies into their strategies. This requires an ongoing commitment to learning and innovation, allowing leaders to leverage technology for enhanced decision-making and improved operational efficiency.

2. *Cultivating a Learning-Oriented Culture:* Creating an organizational culture that prizes learning and knowledge-sharing is vital. Encouraging team members to pursue continuous education and training, and providing the necessary resources to

do so, can foster an environment ripe for innovation and adaptable to change.

3. *Enhancing Emotional Intelligence:* As teams become more diverse and work becomes more decentralized, leaders' emotional intelligence becomes increasingly important. The ability to understand and manage one's own emotions, and to empathize with others, can help navigate the complexities of modern workplace relationships and enhance team cohesion.

4. *Developing Resilience and Flexibility:* The ability to recover from setbacks and adapt to new circumstances is a critical leadership skill, especially in times of uncertainty. Training programs that focus on developing resilience can equip leaders with the tools to maintain stability and confidence, even under pressure.

5. *Strategic Forecasting and Scenario Planning:* Leaders should engage in strategic forecasting and scenario planning to anticipate future trends and potential challenges. This proactive approach allows leaders to prepare for various outcomes and develop flexible strategies that can be adapted as scenarios evolve.

By integrating these strategies into their leadership approach, leaders can ensure they are well-equipped to handle future challenges. The insights and principles distilled in this book aim to not only inspire leaders but also provide them with practical tools to enhance their effectiveness in an ever-changing world. Through a commitment to adaptability, continuous learning, and strategic foresight, leaders can shape the future of their organizations and drive sustained success.

Fostering a Legacy of Leadership: This section delves into how current leaders can effectively pass on their wisdom and expertise to nurture the next generation of leaders. By creating a robust culture of mentorship and thoughtful succession planning, organizations can safeguard and enhance their legacy of effective leadership.

1. *Establishing Mentorship Programs:* One practical approach is to establish formal mentorship programs. These programs should pair seasoned leaders with emerging leaders within the organization. Effective mentorship involves regular one-on-one meetings, goal setting, and the provision of feedback tailored to the mentee's personal and professional development needs.

To ensure success, organizations should provide training for mentors to equip them with the skills needed to guide their mentees effectively.

2. *Creating Pathways for Leadership Development:* Another crucial strategy is the creation of clear pathways for career and leadership development. This can be achieved by identifying and grooming high-potential employees early, offering them tailored training programs, leadership workshops, and rotational assignments across different departments or even geographic locations. These experiences are invaluable in providing emerging leaders with a broader understanding of the organization and its challenges.

3. *Encouraging a Culture of Continuous Learning:* Leaders should cultivate an environment where continuous learning and development are valued. This includes encouraging current leaders to share their knowledge through internal seminars, workshops, and informal lunch-and-learn sessions. Such initiatives not only disseminate valuable knowledge but also foster a sense of community and ongoing engagement among all levels of staff.

4. *Succession Planning:* Effective succession planning is crucial for ensuring that the organization has a ready pool of candidates who can fill key leadership roles as they become available. This process should be transparent and include criteria based on the organization's strategic goals and the specific competencies needed for future leadership roles.

5. *Recognizing and Rewarding Leadership Potential:* Recognize and reward employees who demonstrate leadership potential. This can include formal recognition programs, promotions, or even public acknowledgment of their contributions. Recognition serves as a motivator for future leaders to continue developing their skills and contributing to the organization.

By implementing these strategies, organizations can ensure that their leadership legacy is not only preserved but also strengthened. Investing in the next generation of leaders is crucial for long-term organizational success and resilience.

Vision for Future Leadership: In the closing remarks, we invite readers to envision the future of leadership within their organizations and industries. By embracing the principles of situational leadership and committing to lifelong learning and adaptation, leaders can ensure they are equipped to handle whatever the future holds. We encourage leaders to think strategically about how they can not only apply these principles within their teams but also influence the broader industry or sector.

Closing: As we reflect on the transformative power of situational leadership, we cast our gaze towards the future, envisioning a world where adaptive leadership approaches are the cornerstone of organizational success. By embracing the principles of situational leadership and fostering a culture of innovation and collaboration, leaders can navigate the complexities of the modern workplace with confidence and resilience. As we embark on this transformative journey together, let us seize the opportunity to redefine the future of leadership and unlock the boundless potential that lies within each of us.

Conclusion: Beyond the Horizon

As we conclude our exploration of situational leadership within this book, we find ourselves at a pivotal moment in the evolution of leadership practices. Throughout this journey, we have delved deeply into the transformative power of situational leadership, uncovering its nuances and the significant impact it can have on organizational success. We've explored its fundamental principles and demonstrated how these can be applied effectively in various real-world contexts, equipping leaders with the necessary tools to excel in today's dynamic work environment.

Reflecting on the insights gathered, it is evident that the future of leadership demands flexibility, agility, and responsiveness. In a world characterized by rapid change and complexity, the principles of situational leadership offer a beacon of adaptability, guiding leaders through uncertainty with a strategic and responsive approach. By fostering a culture that values innovation and collaboration, leaders are better prepared to manage the intricacies of the modern workplace, ensuring sustained organizational growth and success.

However, our journey through the landscape of

situational leadership is far from over. As we look ahead, we are presented with the opportunity to further refine and redefine leadership practices. Armed with a deep understanding of situational leadership, we must continue to commit to lifelong learning and growth, embracing change not just as a challenge, but as a catalyst for innovation and progress. Let us harness the collective potential of our teams and organizations, striving together towards a future where adaptive leadership is not just an advantage, but a necessity for thriving in the ever-evolving global marketplace.

Thus, as we move forward, let the enduring principles of situational leadership inspire us to new heights of leadership excellence, driving us to create more resilient and innovative organizations.

Signing off,

Jordan Staub

Acknowledgments

In the journey of bringing this book to fruition, I owe a debt of gratitude to the incredible individuals who have supported and inspired me along the way.

First and foremost, I express my deepest appreciation to my wife, Kyra, whose unwavering love, encouragement, and understanding have been the bedrock of my endeavors. Your boundless patience and steadfast support have sustained me through the challenges and triumphs of this journey, and I am endlessly grateful for your presence in my life.

To my seven children, each of you brings joy, laughter, and endless inspiration to my life. Your boundless curiosity, resilience, and love remind me of the importance of leading with compassion, empathy, and integrity. You are my greatest blessings, and I am immensely proud to be your father.

I am indebted to my mentors, Dr. Siegel, Dr. Schippers and Leylan Mitchell, whose guidance, wisdom, and mentorship have been instrumental in shaping my growth as a leader and scholar. Your unwavering belief in my potential and your willingness to challenge and inspire me have been invaluable gifts on this journey. Thank you for your guidance and support.

I extend my heartfelt gratitude to my colleagues and comrades in both my military and civilian careers. Your camaraderie, professionalism, and dedication to service have enriched my life and shaped my leadership journey in profound ways. Whether in the trenches of the battlefield or the boardrooms of corporate America, I am privileged to have served alongside such exceptional individuals.

Finally, I express my deepest appreciation to the readers of this book. Your curiosity, engagement, and commitment to personal and professional growth inspire me to continue striving for excellence in all that I do. May the insights and lessons shared within these pages empower you on your own leadership journey, and may you continue to navigate the complexities of the modern world with courage, resilience, and integrity.

With heartfelt gratitude,

    Jordan Staub

About the Author:

Jordan Staub is a dynamic leader with a diverse background that is grounded in military service and civilian expertise, distinguished by his unwavering dedication to excellence. Currently serving as an Integrated Logistics Support (ILS) Manager at TACOM - US ARMY, Jordan navigates the complexities of defense logistics with precision and foresight. In addition to his civilian role, he holds the rank of Technical Sergeant (TSGT) in the Michigan Air National Guard, where he serves as a Logistic Management Specialist attached to the 127th Logistics Readiness Squadron (LRS) at Selfridge Air National Base.

Born in Detroit, Michigan, and currently residing in Rochester, MI, Jordan's military journey began with his attachment to the 415th Civil Affairs Battalion (ARMY Reserves) from 2010 to 2013. Since 2013, he has been an integral part of the 127th LRS SQ (Air National Guard), contributing his skills and expertise to various missions and deployments.

Jordan's military assignments include deployments to Operation Enduring Freedom in Kuwait from June 2017 to February 2018, as well as participation in exercises such as Northern Strike and Saber Strike. His invaluable contributions to these missions reflect his commitment to excellence and his ability to lead in high-pressure environments.

Within is civilian career, during his tenure as a Senior Technical Writer and Editor (Publication Manager), Jordan Staub played a pivotal role in developing critical technical materials essential to defense operations, overseeing the creation of technical manuals and other key publications for military weapon systems. His expertise extended beyond documentation, collaborating with supply analysts to forecast and plan for supply demand, ensuring seamless logistical operations. In his capacity as Lead Technical Writer on multiple programs, Jordan provided management, guidance, and oversight on complex weapon system efforts, employing a strategic approach to project management and fostering collaboration among stakeholders to drive mission success. Additionally, he mentored and developed technical writing interns, cultivating a culture of learning and growth within the organization.

Currently serving as the Noncommissioned Officer in Charge (NCOIC) of warehouse operations in the Air National Guard and as an ILS Manager at TACOM, Jordan's leadership is instrumental in ensuring the efficiency and effectiveness of logistical operations.

His strategic vision and commitment to excellence make him a respected leader within the military and civilian sectors alike.

In addition to his military service and civilian career, Jordan is a dedicated scholar, pursuing a Ph.D. in Technology with a specialization in Data Analytics from Walsh College, MI. His passion for continuous learning and his unwavering commitment to excellence exemplify his dedication to both personal and professional growth.

As a leader and scholar, Jordan Staub brings a wealth of knowledge and experience to the realm of leadership and logistics. His collaborative effort in "From Battlefield to Boardroom: Applying Situational Leadership Principles from the Military to Civilian Leadership" reflects his dedication to empowering others to embrace leadership excellence in diverse organizational settings.

From Battlefield to Boardroom

From Battlefield to Boardroom

Made in the USA
Columbia, SC
19 June 2024